Started in the construction industry as an apprentice quantity surveyor in 1965 when he was aged 16, Dave Husband left FIFE in 1971 to work in Liverpool (Merseyside, Cheshire and North Wales).

A naive young Scotsman on a huge learning curve teased by magical scousers. When you are hard up and penniless, humour is still a form of escapism.

He saw first oil ashore in 1978 at Sullom Voe, Shetland. Shetland was a great experience. A special mention to the American coastguards.

Dave worked on contracts all over the United Kingdom. Scotland, England, Wales and Northern Ireland for the next 50 years.

Dealt with "good, bad and sometimes the nasty". He understood the difference between fair and fare!

Dave Husband

American Coastguards, Unst & The B.P. Oily Blacks (1978)

Austin Macauley Publishers
LONDON · CAMBRIDGE · NEW YORK · SHARJAH

Copyright © Dave Husband 2024

The right of Dave Husband to be identified as author of this work has been asserted by the author in accordance with sections 77 and 78 of the Copyright, Designs and Patents Act 1988.

All rights reserved. No part of this publication may be reproduced, stored in a retrieval system, or transmitted in any form or by any means, electronic, mechanical, photocopying, recording, or otherwise, without the prior permission of the publishers.

Any person who commits any unauthorised act in relation to this publication may be liable to criminal prosecution and civil claims for damages.

All of the events in this memoir are true to the best of author's memory. The views expressed in this memoir are solely those of the author.

A CIP catalogue record for this title is available from the British Library.

ISBN 9781035851058 (Paperback)
ISBN 9781035851065 (Hardback)
ISBN 9781035851072 (ePub e-book)

www.austinmacauley.com

First Published 2024
Austin Macauley Publishers Ltd®
1 Canada Square
Canary Wharf
London
E14 5AA

My thanks to my family, friends and former colleagues, who supported me through my life journey, and to the team at Austin Macauley Publishers for their comprehensive proofreading efforts.

I can't remember when I first encountered the young American personnel who were employed at the coastguard base on Shetland, but it was before the first oil shore and before the accommodation ships Rangatira & Stena Baltica appeared at Garth's Voe.

Why were there American coastguards on Shetland? I don't honestly know, but I can remember some lengthy discussions as to what was believed to be their actual function.

Probably the most popular theory amongst our crew was that they were all undercover CIA spies. Whilst I historically sometimes could not see the obvious, if these young people were working undercover for the CIA, they were doing a brilliant job. Dustin Hoffman couldn't have done a better acting job. The coastguards were, in the main, if not all of them, young men. When they were asked a direct question, they confirmed that they were not at liberty to discuss their working environment. All they would confirm was that they played a part in assisting their maritime colleagues.

The coastguard base was located along a remote road from Scatsta airfield. There is a thought that all roads on Shetland are remote. In fairness, there were an awful lot of single-track roads in the 1970s. The coastguard base shut just a few years later.

Scatsta had been the base for 3,000 RAF personnel during the Second World War, including, allegedly, the TV star Hughie Green. Shetland played an especially important part in the Second World War, and the Shetland Bus stories were incredible. The Shetland/Norwegian connection is phenomenal.

I was privileged because I was invited onto the base on a couple of occasions. Whilst there was evidence of security, it was not in any way over the top and did not indicate any major clandestine operation. The perfect background for covert activities? Emphatically no (probably).

There were essentially three Americans amongst their numbers that I became friendly with. Initially, Big Al (Tex), Terry (Dutch), and then latterly Doc. Al was a six-feet-four young Texan in his early 20s, and his nickname was fairly obvious. Terry was a more solid-built young man of a similar age from Pennsylvania and Dutch descent. Once again, his nickname was obvious but in Terry's case, it was used to wind him up, especially by his friends. Al and Terry had been making efforts to socialise with the locals as well as joining the rugby club. Doc, the oldest of the trio, was not interested in the sporting activities but enjoyed the other social activities. Doc, we encountered elsewhere in a different environment. The trio were excellent ambassadors for their country. They weren't shy, quiet individuals by any means, but neither were they loud-mouthed or brash.

I first met the Americans through playing rugby, and the rest of my workmates, apart from the 'Prof.', didn't meet them. The lad's perception of the Yanks was that they were brash and loud-mouthed. The perception, like a lot of things, comes from what we read and the generalisations that we all make as we wander through life.

For me, it was a simple case of taking people as you find them and treating them the way you would want them to treat you.

I had opted to play rugby simply to survive, and looking back, it helped me retain my sanity. It was another step to avoid the Sullom Voe blues. I was never a rugby player, but because of my early working days, I had been persuaded to play for a couple of seasons for the Howe of Fife 4th Fifteen, converting from 'fitba' or soccer, as my American friends would say. Big Al and Terry were not rugby players either but had played American football.

I had played every Saturday, sometimes both morning and afternoon, for ten seasons. My first sporting love was, and remains, soccer.

My old pals would tell you, "I wasn't a 'fitba' player either!"

Even though you accept that you are not the best or anything approaching the best, it doesn't diminish your passion.

The early months on the island were exceedingly difficult simply because there was a lot of tension amongst our team, which occasionally broke out into open hostilities. The unrest and tensions were simply caused by being away from home. Many of the team were not travelling men (Nomads), myself included, and found difficulty adapting or coming to terms with it. Those who did survive still sometimes succumbed to the Sullom Voe blues. It was of the utmost importance that I remained focused in the early months on the reasons I was here. I had a goal.

I decided to put my name down to play for the B.P. Oil Blacks and encountered our American cousins. I did make up the numbers in a couple of games against a contractor, and then a game was arranged against RAF Saxaford on the island of Unst. I would not have considered that option too often because it meant losing money.

It requires two ferries to get to Unst from the main island means taking Saturday off work. I looked forward to visiting the most northerly-inhabited island in Britain. It turned out that the 'Prof.' was also taking the chance to visit the island. The 'Prof.' worked for the same company on a completely different part of the project. The 'Prof.' was a highly intelligent scouse scallywag. The seriously bad news was that the match had now been rearranged, and we were now taking part in a seven-a-side tournament.

B.P. laid on a transit van, and nine of us departed for our rugby tournament in Unst. I knew that I was not fit enough to play in a demanding seven-a-side tournament on a full-sized pitch so did my best to be promoted to one of the reserve positions. I had last played rugby in the 1960s. The trip also allowed me to chat with Al, Terry, and the 'Prof.' The B.P. lad who organised the trip was asking us to remind Al and Terry of the rules of the game! They were used to playing American football and only understood the rudiments of the game! Furthermore, it transpired that six out of the nine wanted to be first or second reserve. The "crack" was worth the trip.

"Crack as in chat, jokes, and wind-ups. Not funny substances."

"Wind-ups as in taking the Michael. Get to Florence."

Abbreviations were to become the normal practice with site paperwork and communications. Not simply a code but a different form of words.

GTF was Get to Florence or Get to France, derived from the old Scots "Get to fuck" and replaced "F off." The Prof. was happy with that. I think Big Al & Terry were bemused but attentive.

When we arrived on Unst, you could see a visible difference from the rest of the Shetland Isles; it was much greener but it was still treeless. The pitch where we were going to play the matches doubled as a soccer pitch and was next to the sea. It's a strange irony that in the Western world, people can find time to build soccer pitches and play games. No matter what hardship or difficulties are faced, we still find time to play.

It turned out that the seven-a-side tournament was cancelled because none of the other teams could afford the time off work or had managed to make the trip. There was a general air of disappointment, even though most of us had voiced concerns about playing. However, the RAF had fifteen players who wanted to play, and an effort was made to recruit from the ranks of the spectators. It was a military-type recruitment by one of their senior personnel.

"I want three volunteers. You, you, and you."

When I looked back, I often wondered why only three were recruited, and it remains a mystery! The match started with a full-strength Saxaford fifteen versus B.P. Oil Blacks twelve. We must have been mad to start with three men short. I think there was a gentleman's agreement to give us a man if it was no contest!

"Three men short from a fool team."

They were difficult times for the military, and there was still a possible threat from the Russians. Ronald Reagan was still in serious nuclear disarmament talks, and there were all kinds of NATO exercises going on. The game was an exercise in military tactics.

Always ensure that the opposition is under strength before you start, as it seriously increases your chances of winning. However, never put all your faith in military tactics. It would have been fair to assume that the three squaddies who were seconded to play for us were dumplings. Nothing could be further from the truth. The three of them played with a fervour and passion that comes from the inner soul when you have been rejected by those who think you are not good enough. I thought they had been press-ganged, so how did we have this scenario? I said to one of them, a red-haired fiery-looking character, "I thought you weren't interested in playing."

His response was, "Not for that snobbish bastard," pointing at one of the opposition, who was apparently an officer. The popularity of leadership!

It made for an interesting team talk. There was no game plan, and now we had to sort out what positions we were going to play. Al and Terry just took it in their stride. The B.P. organiser and our team captain took it upon himself to do the motivating team talk.

"Let's hit them hard but fair and let's be first to the loose balls. Let's show them we mean business."

One of the seconded recruits piped up, "Let's fuck them."

"Apologies, but sometimes you tell it the way it was." GTF was not appropriate at this time, and I thought this was going to be a friendly game!

We played with 5 or 6 forwards up front in the pack. Terry, solid as he was, packed at prop forward in the front row. Al was a natural for the second row and two of the recruits played in the pack. There was no quarter being given in the forward battle. I played as scrum half, and the Prof. played as fullback.

The technicalities of the game were causing Dutch and Tex some problems. Dutch bore the brunt of the pain in his neck and shoulders, partly because Tex was too big. Dutch was asking for assistance, and his second-row partner explained, "You've got to bend your knees, Tex, and push Dutch straight up his arse."

This was a word that wasn't in Tex's vocabulary. There was sufficient knowledge of American movies to come up with alternatives such as butt or fanny. The pain never subsided for Dutch, but I believe it didn't get any worse. When the opposition realised there were a couple of Americans, it did create a couple of side issues. However, the biggest problem was that at one stage, Dutch and Tex thought they were playing American football. In rugby, you must go for the man with the ball, but they were taking men off the ball. It was hilarious to watch the unbelievable nervousness it caused amongst the opposition. They were trying to keep one eye on the ball but also keeping a wary eye on our American duo. Tex flattened a couple of their players, and their concentration was affected. I had a sneaking suspicion that the referee was not unaware but maybe allowed us a little latitude because of the numbers.

During a passage of play, Tex's tackle on one of their players resulted in the tackled player sustaining a broken ankle. It was a fair tackle and a genuine accident.

One of our recruits piped up, "It evens up the numbers, big man."

There is no answer to that, but it was an accident. (I think!)

The remainder of the game continued uneventfully and ended in a draw. Our three recruits probably got the greatest pleasure. I was totally knackered and just relieved to hear the final whistle. Terry and Al, alias Dutch/Tex, had enjoyed the encounter. In military terms, they had limited our resources but learnt another lesson. Know your enemy and remember that those who feel they have been dealt with unfairly will fight like hell. It was now time to unwind and retire to the bar.

There was something perverse in 28 grown men, including the referee, chasing an oval ball around the most northerly-inhabited island in the British Isles.

The RAF had a large Anderson shelter appropriately named the Penguin Club, which doubled as a social club with a bar. Only when we were on the point of demobilising to the social club were we made aware that we had missed the last ferry connection and, by default, we would have to spend the night on the island. It also meant that you missed the next day at work, which would make it an even more expensive weekend.

A couple of the lads with the B.P. connections who were in married quarters had to make hurried phone calls home. Spell popular!

At least we did not have to pay for accommodation because we were to be billeted in the RAF camp.

Anyway, I digress, but we were just wandering into the salubrious surroundings of the Penguin Club. It was one of those places where you would not normally take your dog to relieve itself, but we were undoubtedly a captive audience.

Although the team was not old, there were no youngsters. The Prof. was winding up the Americans (Big Al & Terry), and I was picking up the scraps.

There was one female in the club who I believe was one of the RAF officer's fiancée. She was the centre of attraction only until those who were interested realised that she was unavailable, and normal services were resumed. The presence of the female fraternity usually brought decorum to the proceedings or at least curbed the worst excesses.

The Prof.'s days were numbered because he did not suffer fools gladly and was not a member of our leader's fan club. He had somewhat elegantly described him at one of the team-building exercises as a Merchant Banker (a slang version for one who participates in self-abuse). The Prof. did not follow the Scouse Sycophant School of Philosophy.

He was nevertheless vulnerable, like many of us, and very funny with his acid wit. The world is full of funny Scousers who are not so keen on make-believe people. Our leader had entered an unreal world inhabited by a lot of unreal people, and as a result, was caught in a surreal situation. He could not distinguish the sincere from the insincere, and to ensure survival, you must be subservient to the main B.P. man.

All we were going to do was drink a few pints and enjoy ourselves.

The Prof. said to Tex standing at the bar.

"Hey La, I can see right up your nostrils."

Tex stood some 10–12 inches taller than the Prof. There was no quick riposte, just a furrowed brow from Tex.

Tex replied, "Hey man, you talk funny."

The Prof. retorted, "Just what I was thinking, La."

Tex suggested, "Speak slowly, boy."

The Prof. replied, "From here, I can see up your nostrils."

Tex asked, "You want a closer look."

The Prof. joked, "As long as we can hold hands at the same time."

Terry remarked, "Al, I think this is going to be a long night."

It was also entertaining!

The early part of the evening entertainment in the Penguin Club was both informative and entertaining.

It was a meeting of different people from different cultural backgrounds: Military service personnel, construction workers, and various ancillary industry workers, plus, the two American lads.

The Prof. and I were straightforward inquisitive.

What was RAF Saxaford? What did they do?

There was no airstrip and, therefore, no aeroplanes. There was a small airstrip for the local civil service Loganair. There was also a helicopter landing strip servicing the North Sea oil fields.

RAF Saxaford was essentially a listening station, and to the extent of it, we had no idea. There were a couple of large domes on the hill, and we had no idea of the number of personnel involved.

I don't remember anyone giving us specific information or telling us anything seriously illuminating. Historically, we have a lot to thank the RAF for, and in our modern world, they still play a large part in our overall defence strategy.

The derogatory remarks/comments by our colleagues from down south about Shetland and Sullom Voe were repeated in RAF terminology about Saxaford.

The Prof. said, "Shetland was the arsehole of the British Isles, and Sullom Voe was two-thirds up."

I said, "I think you mean two turds."

The Prof. replied, "That's what I said."

I said, "No, Tex thought you were discussing fractions. He does not know the difference between a turd and a third with your Scouse accent."

The Prof. said, "Tell him that this fraction is a pile of SH."

Interrupting, "Sugar." Could I get a job as a translator?

The Prof. asked, "Talking of sugar, Tex, they tell me that you are a big Bond fan?"

Tex & Terry responded, "Sean Connery."

The Prof. was in full flow now. Rumours, half-truths, and statistics were all part of this project. I first heard Winston Churchill quoting one of Mark Twain's sayings. There are lies, damned lies, & statistics. Oh, how true.

The Prof. added, "Did you know that Sean was a milk boy, in the Navy, and before becoming a film star, a Shetland Sugar Salesman?"

I remember thinking that I did not know that. Milk Boy and Navy, yes. My naive brain did not kick into gear once again. Start with a truth, and the embellished story gains credence.

Terry said, "There may be people here who remember him?"

I remembered that the Prof. had a wee skill of imitating Mr Connery.

Mr Connery was an impressionist's dream voice.

The Prof. imitated, "You can just hear him, Terry/Tex. My name is Shaun!

"Shaun Connery, your Shetland Shugar Shalesman!"

It was lost on Terry, but he then said, "My dad worked for Tate & Lyle. I wonder if their paths ever crossed."

The Prof. replied, "Not in Shetland, Terry. Shaun worked for Shilver Shpoon."

I resisted a GTF after I stopped laughing. Who was to know that Sean would be knighted further down the line? I can see that on a business card, and the Prof. reading it.

> **"Shur Shaun."**
> **"Shetland Shugar Shalesman."**
> **"Shilver Shpoon."**

How do the two turds relate to RAF Saxaford?

Well, in RAF circles, a Saxaford posting was considered to be a black mark on your career prospects. Therefore, it was considered to be the arsehole of the world.

I'm sure that was not true of all the personnel, but as with the Sullom Voe construction contract, there were a lot of ancillary operatives, from cooks and cleaners to bakers, but maybe not candlestick makers. Tinkers, tailors, soldiers, sailors, and maybe spies.

We had an informative and humorous conversation about infiltration into their RAF world and the steps they took to combat security breaches. Mick and RAF corporal reckoned their island network was pretty extensive, and as soon as a stranger was spotted on the ferry, they were immediately informed. You could always spot the Russians because they wore funny hats!

I remember thinking that nine strangers had got on the ferry to purportedly play rugby, and I don't remember any checks being made to verify our status. Like any military establishment in the provinces, they probably did not have too many security problems or scares. There were some horrendous terrorist attacks taking place on mainland Britain, but the northern part, including Scotland and all the islands, had largely escaped the terrorism. In fairness, we were not near any sensitive areas like the domes on the hill, if in fact, they were sensitive areas.

Around 1979, we did have an alleged Scottish terrorist and former bank robber working with us for a month on the process plot. He just never returned from leave.

The Prof. told the story about the Russian spy being parachuted into the north of Scotland or Shetland. We then got into a conversation about the possibility of someone being parachuted in and the more doubt we could put into Mick's head. More pints and more alcohol were consumed. It is fair to say that the night was heating up, and the banter continued apace.

The Prof. said, "Let me share a story with you, a Russian Spy Story.

The Russians were training this spy long before the demolition of the Berlin Wall to be parachuted into the north of Scotland. The last piece of advice that he was given was whatever he did, not to get into an argument about religion.

He was advised that probably the best form of defence was just to say that you were the same. So, if the person you meet is a Catholic, Presbyterian, Congregationalist, etc., just concur.

In fact, in the outback, you may encounter some of the minority religions such as Wee Frees or Closed Brethren, once again just go with the flow.

Unfortunately, when the eventful drop took place, the Russian spy was blown miles off course and ended up in the wilds."

Mick asked, "Shetland?"

The Prof. replied, "Could be. So, the first person the Russian meets is a hippy shepherd."

Mick nodded, "Quite a big hippy community up here."

The Prof. continued, "Yes. So the spy introduces himself and asks the shepherd who he is." "The shepherd," the Prof. narrated, "in soft lilting Highland accent, says, 'The name is McLeod, Hamish McLeod'."

The Russian spy, now intrigued, was suddenly aware that he is not tuned to all the differing accents but asked the shepherd what he is and what he does.

Mick nodded his head.

The Prof. concluded, "The shepherd, pausing, thinks it's a funny question and decides to tell it as it is. (In his soft brogue) 'Well, actually, I'm a homosexual shepherd'."

The Russian hadn't a clue what he had said but responded by his training, "Well, I'm just the same."

The moral of the story, Mick, is, "A Red Spy at Night is a Shepherd's Delight."

The evening was going well.

The Prof. asked, "Mick, did you know that Mick Jagger and the Rolling Stones immortalised that Russian spy in 1965 in a song? It became a number-one hit. 'Get off of McLeod'."

Mick, the RAF corporal, remembered the song as well.

"Hey, Hey You, You, Get off of My Cloud."

We all started singing.

One of the good things with the rugby crowd is that you always got a good singsong, although some of the choruses were not for the prudish or easily offended.

The same idea was in the old days when there was a piano, and there would be a sing-along. You do need a couple of extroverts or at least people who are a little less inhibited because they've got a couple of drinks in them.

I remember thinking that I would have to come back one day if I got a chance to visit the island. Although I never came back to play rugby, I did return on three separate occasions.

"Nostalgia is a wonderful thing."

"Anyway, I think the Prof. was not gay, but he could play camp when it suited him and also wind people up to leave an element of doubt."

There was no hidden agenda, just straightforward humour to make life a wee bit more bearable.

Strangely, when I stayed at Toft camp in the early days, I can remember meeting two lads, one from my old school, who I found out were partners. It is always nice to see a friendly old face and have a blether. It was not quite as simple as that, and one of them was distinctly nasty. However, that is for another time.

Tex and Terry were a little bit disappointed, I seem to recollect because there was going to be no opportunity for them to meet any members of the fairer sex simply because there weren't very many!

What does the working man or woman discuss when they are thrown together coming from completely different working environments?

Money, conditions, sport, politics, sex, and possibly religion would all be discussed at various times, although not necessarily in that order until the serious drinking kicked in at the end of the evening when the singing took over completely.

So, we had a Scouser, a Jock, a Texan, a Pennsylvanian Dutch, and Mick, who was an Essex Boy.

I can't remember the monetary figures, but I can remember thinking if Mick was telling us the truth, the lower ranks in the armed forces were poorly paid in 1978. The conditions, including living conditions and travel, were not particularly spectacular. Four years later, they were to be in the Falklands and all that entailed. The morale was low.

A year later, we were going to be discussing Maggie's millions (i.e., the reference to the increased unemployed blamed on Mrs Thatcher).

Construction workers generally did not have particularly good living conditions, but Sullom Voe was an exception. The travel arrangements were also good, but getting off and on the island could be hazardous due to the fog rolling off the sea. You could be stuck for a couple of days, and that just came off your leave.

Tex and Terry were just proud to be American citizens. They were proud to hold the American passport and paid for that privilege. The general American public only got 2 weeks' holiday a year, and they just accepted that they had a tour of duty. They weren't brainwashed or anything silly like that. They were two likeable young men who appeared generally to be happy with their lot. I remember a book published in the late '50s by an American author, which castigated the Americans for their public relations, and also anything that was faintly communist. They were, therefore, as a result, not necessarily one of the most popular nationalities in the world.

Tex said that for all their unpopularity, there was still a tremendous number of people from all the Latin American countries, including Mexico, trying to get into the U.S.A. He had a greater insight into that coming from Texas. Just 3 years later, in 1981, I was in Florida and read all the reports of the boat people from the Caribbean Islands, including Cuba. It would have been nice to catch up with Tex & Terry.

The British were able to understand worldwide unpopularity when they chose to defend the Falkland Isles. Our colonial history puts us top at the top of the popularity polls!

My father had worked in Boston in the 1920s and 1930s.

I had the good fortune to have worked and lived in Merseyside and was still living on the periphery of Merseyside. It had humour, hardship, football, and the Beatles. They had that whole Mersey sound in the 1960s.

The Prof. and I were able to relate to many of the subjects of discussion that evening in early 1978. I had worked beside a lad whose partner was a relative of the Beatles' road manager, Mal Evans, who was shot in the States in January 1976. He had performed on the Sgt. Pepper's album also had a cameo role in Help.

It gave me some street credibility with Prof., Tex, and Terry, although I think we had lost Mick because he was beginning to worry about parachutists and shepherds!

Security is twenty-four hours a day, seven days a week. There is not truly any situation that is fail-safe.

Terror is sowing a seed. It is a form of blackmail. We had only been joking, but we had not truly been attempting to offend. There were two incidents related to armed forces and an ex-terrorist, which had still not happened in 1978 before the visit to Unst.

For some, the word "terrorist" was synonymous with the word "freedom fighter." For others, it was another word for "criminal" or "anarchist." I have never believed that you can truthfully decommission a terrorist. I was working on a contract in middle England, Stratford-upon-Avon, when the two Birmingham pub bombs were detonated in November 1974, just a few years before this moment, killing twenty-one mainly young people. I had been in one of the pubs the week before, not far from New Street railway station, and strongly adhered to the saying, "If you are in the wrong place at the wrong time or the right place at the right time."

I was travelling down from North Wales to Stratford on the train two or three times a month during this period, and naturally, the 'Brummies' were suspicious of my accent after this appalling incident. It was just different and not local. Scottish but not Irish.

Six Irish suspects were arrested and convicted, but many years later were exonerated and pardoned. There remained no justice for the many families that had suffered loss.

Some terrorists simply grow old, and are we ever going to defeat some of the senseless acts? Unfortunately, there is no clear-cut answer.

We were trapped on the island for the evening, and the only thing to do was make the best of it.

From the Penguin Club, we demobilised to the Sergeant's Mess.

I had never been in a Sergeant's Mess before, and it was a lot of years later before I was to be back inside another one, so I cannot claim expertise, but undoubtedly it was or is a unique institution. It was enthralling to see the workings of this type of organisation.

I think the drink was inexpensive, but you had to go through the appropriate channels to order drinks. It looked like tables were allocated to specific RAF personnel, and they had their little cliques. There was a sergeant who I did not recognise who had played in the match. We seemed to aspire to his table.

He was telling a couple of young privates of his exploits during the match and how there had been a couple of Yanks playing for the B.P. team. He showed them what for. "They did not beat us!" They broke an officer's ankle! In fairness, it wasn't a lie but not the way we would have reported the match!

I don't think Tex & Terry heard the conversation. Sometimes with accents, there is still a language barrier.

The Prof. did hear and said, "An Occifer, not all bad news."

I remember thinking, "Occifer, it is better than GTF." No way was the Prof. ever going to win diplomat of the year.

The evening was not going downhill, but it was slowing down. The Sullom Voe Blues did not kick in, but you realise that you would far rather be somewhere else.

The Prof. and I were not on the same wavelength, but as with so many other cases on the project, merely ships passing in the night. The banter continued with our American teammates, although Mick had wandered off somewhere else.

Our night did not end in the Sergeant's mess. We were invited to the Baltasound Hotel for a nightcap. We all piled into the transport and headed the short distance to the Unst hotel. I don't believe that the lad who was driving the van was drunk, but I honestly don't know if he would have failed a breathalyser, but it was not viewed as a problem.

However, there had been a few of our workmates stopped by the local constabulary and subsequently lost their driving licences as a consequence of failing the breath test. Stan the man had given me the lecture about one of the good lads from the Vadil who had got caught doing a favour. Sadly, in 1978, some 11 years after the drink-driving act was passed, that was still our thought for a large majority of us, "Getting caught." The Construction Industry had more than its fair share of one for the road.

The breathalyser had been introduced in 1967 and was now this decade starting to be enforced, as noted at the site. However, here on Unst, as per many Scottish islands, there was no local policeman. A difficult law to enforce, although there is never a defence.

The Baltasound Hotel is the most northerly in the U.K. I visited it in the twenty-first century and enjoyed a family lunch. I had forgotten that it is only a small hotel.

When we visited the hotel later after the Penguin Club and the Sergeants Mess, there was a Shetland wedding reception in full swing. Tex and Terry were not quite dumbstruck, but there was a lot to take on board. The Prof. was in his element, but one of the other lads managed to bring decorum to the ongoings.

It appeared to be a happy occasion, and thankfully our intrusion did not bring any negativity to the event. I don't remember the Shetland fiddlers on this occasion. There was a piano being played and a variety of songs being sung. I'm not blaming the Prof., but I seem to remember someone starting with the first line of "Dinah, Dinah, show us your leg," and someone else bellowing "Whoa."

Popular music covers continents. Terry and Tex could join in with "Hey Jude, Nah, Nah, Nah, Nana, Nah, Hey Jude." The evening was drawing to a close. We just needed Simon and Garfunkel to sing "Homeward Bound." It was not too expensive a day, but the reflection was for tomorrow.

We got the shout "Back to the transport." We were being billeted by the RAF in their Saxaford camp. I can just hear the Prof. "And now for bed," said Zebedee.

We had to be grateful. It came at no additional expense, and we got a cooked breakfast the next morning. Some of us are easily pleased. I remember thinking I'll not be back here again. However, I did visit Unst again a further three times. Once in the twenty-first century, but the base shut in 2006.

The only time I can remember Tex and Terry having words (not fighting) was that peaceful Sunday morning. For some reason, they had been in the same bed. It got quite heated until Tex realised he got out of his bed in the middle of the night to visit the toilet and just climbed back into the nearest bed. Raised voices but no bad language. Tex was just a big gentle giant. The Prof. was still with Zebedee.

The journey back to Mainland Shetland, across two ferries, was fairly uneventful. The smell emanating from inside the transport, however, would have given a combined scientific and sewerage department unique challenges. Could they have added another gas discovery to the periodic table?

Although the Prof. and I worked for the same company, our paths never crossed workwise. I played a few games of rugby and several games of five-a-side football. The two construction camps, Firth and Toft, had excellent facilities.

There was a lot of tension in the early days between various factions in the group and a fair bit of turnover of personnel. The Prof. never had a "leaving do." He just disappeared.

The friendship with the American lads was, for me, a welcome diversion from some of the internal shenanigans. They had a job to do, but they were still happy to meet some of the outside world. I was impressed by the whole team.

As far as I can remember, Tex and Terry were a couple of single lads and were keen, wherever possible, to meet girls. It was exceedingly difficult for them as they were in the serious minority, but it never stopped them from trying.

Through visits to their base, I met one of the senior coastguards and also one of their bosses.

It turned out Doc, the senior coastguard, had a partner, and they were also happy to participate in activities that took them away from the normal mundane daily duties. Doc was not interested in rugby but was happy to get involved with Tex & Terry when there were other potential social activities on the horizon.

Doc appeared at the Brae Hotel after one of our rugby matches, and we just got chatting. They must have wondered a little bit about the atmosphere. The matches got a bit more competitive. There was big Archie and a couple of fiery Welsh lads that could handle all the physical stuff. They were proud to show their wounds. The wonderful thing about rugby is that there is usually no-nonsense after the final whistle. The singing was still boisterous and irreverent as the night wore on. Tex and Terry had become acclimatised. Doc and his partner appeared to be enthralled. The just sat and listened.

"Cosher Bailey had an engine that was always needing mending.

And when at full power, it did five miles per hour.

Did you ever see such a funny thing before?"

I heard about Auntie Annie, Brother Daniel, and many other verses.

The irreverent version of "Rule Britannia" was not universally appreciated by everyone but was not out of place in the Shetlands.

"Rule Britannia, Marmalade or Jam.

Five Chinese crackers up your arsehole,

Bang, Bang, Bang, Bang, Bang."

I do not think the Doc could truly comprehend the apparent disrespect to the country in singing this irreverent version of the song. The subsequent discussions covered topics like freedom, Anarchy, and democracy.

The Doc was not arrogant, just laid back, and carried more than a hint of mischievous fun. Tex and Terry addressed him as "Doc," and so did his partner. I remember asking him, "What was his name short for?" Thinking that he was simply a doctor.

Terry said, "Tell him the story, Doc."

Doc said, "The name is Welby, as in Doc Welby, the television series."

I confirmed that I had seen the programme on British television.

Terry said, "Tell him the full story."

Silent thought "Engage Brain." Maybe just a different fool story.

Doc said, "My last posting was on Marcus Island in the Pacific."

I unashamedly never heard of it. The name of the doctor on the television show was Marcus Welby, and therefore, by some divine ritual, the Doc had correctly inherited the nickname.

My research subsequently confirmed that Marcus Island was a real place and had played a significant role in the history of the Second World War.

I do not know how long the Doc was stationed on the island, but it was a different posting from Shetland. It had been a part of Japan's defence during the Second World War, and there was still a Japanese squad on the island.

There was still a bit of bad feeling between the two different nationalities, and no room for socialising. Not shocking because I can remember there was still a little of that anti-Japanese feeling in the United Kingdom because of the treatment of the British prisoners of war.

The talk was about boycotting Japanese cars, etc.

It was just a chance to hear different opinions/viewpoints from ordinary American people. No brainwashing. I often wondered about Doc's actual expertise and if the move from Marcus Island was voluntary.

He retold a story of fighting with the Japanese on the island and various communications passing between them.

Doc said, "They wanted to organise a raiding party on the Japanese premises because of the alleged secretive movement of unknown personnel.

"Just a few years before, there had been a couple of Japanese soldiers found hiding in the Philippine forests some 29 years after the war had ended. To find another one would have put us on the map."

The world loves or hates conspiracy stories. Some 30 years after the war had ended, some nerves were still raw.

Doc continued, "We were charging their premises, shouting Banzai, Banzai.

"They were shouting back, Member Pel Harba!

"Unfortunately, one or two of our older colleagues did remember Pearl Harbour."

I said, "No guns or firearms involved?"

Doc replied, "No, just brooms, brushes, and booze bottles."

I asked, "What happened?"

Doc replied, "Diplomacy kicked in. We got our knuckles rapped."

When the insults were flying, Hiroshima and Nagasaki were mentioned. It's not something you can joke about and a couple of the darkest few days in the world's history.

The discussion on Hiroshima and Nagasaki came at a later date over a cup of coffee and a game of pool.

Doc was interested in experiencing some of our camp life and a break from their routine. There were accommodation problems on the island, and there was talk of a small number of us starting to commute from Glasgow three days a week. However, he had heard about the cabaret nights that were being organised for the Firth and Toft camps.

I did not do a lot of the cabaret nights. They featured older pop stars, comedians, and various variety acts. There was nothing wrong with the acts, but many times the night deteriorated into a drunken rabble. The acoustics in Toft were not the best, considering there were approximately four hundred men and thirty women. You had to admire some of the performers for their ability to manipulate difficult situations.

I had not turned into a hermit but was being more prudent with my money. I had also decided to have alcohol-free nights. Being sober meant I had to take my turn at driving. You couldn't admit to having a book to read.

We managed to get a table for 8 or 10 people. There was Tex, Terry, Doc, and his partner, Kathy, along with a few of my colleagues. The good news was that Tex had met a young lady who worked as a Cost Engineer on the project. I honestly do not know how the friendship worked out, but it was a welcome addition for Tex. After all, he was a tall and handsome young man.

Del Shannon was one of the cabaret acts. He was well-known because he had a number one record in the States. There was a sufficient age group who remembered him fondly. He did well and was still in good shape. Ultimately, he was doing the same as the rest of us, trying to earn a living.

Doc and Kathy knew who Del Shannon was but might have been touched with a bit of sadness to see him performing in this big shed in Shetland. They were big fans of Elvis, who had passed away the year before in 1977. The tribute acts were just starting.

I remember thinking that at least Del was still working.

He brought happiness to quite a few people that Shetland night, and you cannot criticise him for that. He was still recording music at this time and making LPs, but apparently, he had an alcohol problem. He was on the wagon at this moment in time, and the construction industry could understand that problem. Sadly, he committed suicide a few years after this in 1990.

Later that night, I think Doc and Kathy danced at some stage during the proceedings. Country and Western was also extremely popular. The good thing was many of the songs were popular on both sides of the Atlantic. Singalongs became extremely popular.

Johnnie Cash's songs were popular, and the acts soon learnt the words to his many hits. Definitely, the most popular song was a parody of his song "Folsom Prison Blues," appropriately named "The Sullom Voe Blues."

I just heard, "I hear the freight train coming."

Sullom Voe was not a prison, but there was a downside which brought on the blues. There were no trains in Shetland.

Tex, Terry, Doc, and Kathy had all enjoyed the evening. Enjoyed a few chats afterwards, but I was beginning to work longer hours, and survival remained my priority.

Doc was inquisitive to learn about my family and more about our way of life. Equally, I was more than happy to listen to his views/opinions. Although I have read a few American authors, it still amazes me how much we were influenced by American television and films.

It did not just start in Shetland, but I was able to tell Doc that I was full of useless information.

I told him, "My dad was due to sail to the States in autumn 1939 on board the passenger ship SS. Athenia, which was sailing out of the Clyde. He decided to cancel the trip, and the ship was subsequently sunk by a German U-boat two days after the war was declared."

Doc knew about the Athenia, and he had read somewhere that a young future president, JFK, had visited Glasgow to tell the future travellers that if they sailed in ships in 1939 that were flying the American flag, they would be safe. That incident didn't bring the United States into the war, but you can understand the American reluctance to be involved in another European war just two decades after the first.

Doc admired the Queen, but the American public did not want the head of state to be a monarch. He did not believe in inherited privilege but I accepted that there was a huge fascination when the tourists visited London.

For me, I was not particularly anti-monarchy, but I had to admit the inherited privilege angle was wearing thin.

A year after his death, Elvis was still well-remembered. I was not a huge fan but preferred his earlier works. He gave an awful lot of pleasure to a lot of people. The three deaths that I remembered from the previous decade were JFK, Bobby Kennedy, and Martin Luther King.

Doc said, "These are not proud moments in our history."

I do not remember any racial issues. The coastguards were multiracial. The Doc informed me that there were over three hundred Native Red Indian American tribes. The indigenous people did not necessarily do too well, as he reminded me. I remember thinking but did not say to Doc that the Aborigines and Maori had problems in the Southern Hemisphere.

Cowboy films were becoming less popular. Red Indians were usually portrayed as the baddies, while the cowboys were the goodies. The Lone Ranger changed that a little bit because his Red Indian sidekick, Tonto, was a goodie. I reminded Doc of a great line from one of the old film scripts.

Red Indian chief to John Wayne, "White man speak with forked tongue."

Doc commented, "Not a lot of changes."

Doc also informed me that there was an alleged incident with one of their teams at the base. A new runway was being constructed at Scatsca next to the coastguard's base, and someone had stolen one of the large diggers and taken it for a joy ride. Surprisingly, no one was charged.

There was some friction between the relevant parties involved in the fracas, but it was quickly resolved when news broke about a big NATO exercise that was to happen shortly.

If my memory serves me correctly, the NATO exercise was in the summer of 1978 before the first oil reached shore. My accommodation was a three-bedroomed mid-terrace house in Mossbank village, not far from the Firth construction camp. I never discussed NATO with Doc, but undoubtedly the Coastguards were involved. We were told that there were approximately 40,000 operatives taking part.

One of my work colleagues, Roger, whom I shared the accommodation, had arranged a party through his sailing connections. I witnessed a UFO early one morning on my way to work in the middle of the NATO exercise but did not believe it was aliens. It was a big black machine of some kind that appeared to fly about a few hundred feet above sea level. I don't remember seeing wings on this black machine, but it happened so fast. The Doc would have had an opinion on this flying machine, but I'm not sure he would be too concerned. It was almost certainly an American Flying machine.

The party did happen, although the Coastguards were not in attendance. There were three Army Paratroopers who turned up, but, like with the majority of parties connected to the Construction contract, there were very few females in attendance. The three gentlemen were disappointed, but what was probably more worrying was that one of them was acting very strangely. He had been involved in a serious incident whilst on duty, and the two other lads now acted as his chaperones. When he started drinking, he reminded me of my alcoholic Power Station Cost Engineer pal. I knew there was potentially going to be a problem, but his two mates intervened, and they escorted him away from the party before things got out of hand. He looked in a dreadful shape, and goodness knows what had happened to him.

There were a couple of nurses who worked at the camps and were involved in the same company of friends of Roger. I can always remember one of them telling us that she had recently transferred from the Mater Hospital in Northern Island. She had some sad stories to tell, but thankfully she was not at the same party as our Paratrooper friends. I never knew if the two were connected, but I did wonder. A decade later, I was working on a contract at the Mater Hospital as a subcontractor to Laing Construction. No unhappy memories.

We also had major incidents happening in Mainland Britain, specifically Northern England, in the late 70s. Young women were being murdered by a man that the press had christened as "The Yorkshire Ripper." It had been revealed that "The Ripper" had been making mocking phone calls to the police, and he had a very strong Geordie accent. We were allowed to hear part of one of the recordings on a television programme. There were a fair number of operatives on the Sullom Voe contract who had a Geordie accent, and some of the Power Station operatives thought it sounded like one of CJB's Cost Engineers. We were subsequently informed that there had been an alleged rape on the island, and every male operative was interviewed. However, there were no confirmations that anyone had been charged with rape. It was also established that our Cost Engineer colleague was not a suspect. It was one of the lines of thought that "The Ripper" may have worked in the Construction Industry.

"The Yorkshire Ripper" was caught in 1981, and he was not a Geordie. The person making the telephone calls was a hoaxer. It's really sad to think of the individual who knowingly diverted important resources. Computer technology was still in its infancy, and the updated modern systems would have brought the conclusion quicker.

I never discussed the Yorkshire Ripper story with Doc; the topic just did not come in our conversations. We discussed all sorts of other things, including American movie stars.

Clint Eastwood was undoubtedly one of the biggest stars of that era and was guaranteed to fill the camp cinemas. He was popular on both sides of the Atlantic, and we could discuss his brilliant career.

"Rawhide," "A Fistful of Dollars," "Dirty Harry," and "The Good, The Bad and The Ugly." The Dirty Harry films.

I remembered "Rowdy Yates" with affection. The name conjured up a different memory for me, which I knew Doc would not understand, but I still had to run it by him.

"Doc, I can remember when Rowdy Yeats signed for Liverpool."

Doc asked, "Liverpool?"

"Liverpool F.C., Doc. Football." I replied.

Doc said, "Soccer? Clint Eastwood never played soccer!"

I said, "Socca! Socca! No. Football! Football. Not Clint but Rowdy.

"Actually, big Ron Yeats, nicknamed Rowdy."

I needed someone like the Prof. to explain to Doc, but I remembered that the Prof. was an Evertonian, and he would have just gone deaf.

The explanation was lost. Big Ron, also known as Rowdy, was a six-foot-two Aberdonian who signed for Liverpool in the early sixties and was their first captain to lift the FA Cup.

Soccer still had not travelled big time west across the Atlantic.

In the late 1950s and early 1960s, six-foot-two was big for a Scotsman. There had still been rationing after the Second World War in the 1950s, and Rickets had still been prevalent in many parts of Scotland.

John Belushi and Dan Ackroyd were also amongst the names discussed.

"The Blues Brothers" film was still to be shot. They were also to shoot a less successful surreal comedy, "1941."

It was strange that we had discussed Pearl Harbor at a previous meeting. I do not know how, but Hiroshima and Nagasaki were brought into the conversation.

I told Doc that in 1963, I had a CND badge (Campaign for Nuclear Disarmament) that had been stolen. There had been no great deep thinking behind wearing the badge, just a young man courting rebellion and maybe a wee bit of posing.

Doc responded, "I am for disarmament, but it must be multilateral. The long-term consequences of Hiroshima and Nagasaki are just beyond comprehension."

I asked, "So, was it the wrong decision, Doc?"

Doc replied, "No, Harry Truman's decision with the Allies' agreement saved hundreds and thousands of American lives. In a war situation, the priority is saving your people. I do not know how much warning the Japs got about the first bomb, but the second bomb at Nagasaki was three days later."

I asked, "Were they talking, though?"

Doc said, "I believe so. Nagasaki could have been avoided."

I inquired, "Can we achieve the nuclear ban?"

Doc responded, "Can we trust people? Remember your CND badge was stolen."

J. Robert Oppenheimer, the man credited with being the inventor of the atomic bomb, had died the previous decade, in 1967. He realised that the next generations had to deal with future serious potential problems.

We had just been joined by one of the Coastguard Bosses' wives, Barbara. The conversation returned to Del Shannon and Elvis. We were just sitting and enjoying our cups of coffee.

Barbara was a heavy smoker and a little bit suspicious of me. I was not worried, but I had found the higher echelons in the Coastguard fraternity were wary of outsiders, which was perfectly understandable. Maybe I should stop wearing that funny hat that Mick had spoken about at RAF Saxaford!

Barbara gave me a prediction for my future, which turned out to be untrue, and it would have been nice to have reminded her.

Barbara said, "You will never work for an American employer because American employers do not trust non-smokers."

Could have done with the Prof. giving 'Babs' some scouse repartee, but I just shrugged my shoulders. I had not heard that before, and I have not heard of it since. The tobacco industry was immensely powerful in the twentieth century.

In the 1980s, I worked on a Cryogenic Storage contract with a company called Liquified Energy Gas Systems with

Pittsburgh-Des Moines connections. Gerry and Fred, my two American colleagues, never asked if I smoked.

I cannot remember when Tex, Terry, and Doc's tour of duty was ending, but there were serious accommodation problems on the site. That first year, I was in camp at Mossbank, Glasgow, and then back to one of the Accommodation Boats that was anchored in Garth's Voe.

There was another famous American who had died in 1975, who my parents had been great fans of, and that was Paul Robeson. He had toured England and Scotland in the 1920s, 1930s, and 1940s. After the Second World War, I was telling Barbara that my dad had worked in the States, specifically Boston, in the 1920s and early 30s.

My parents had loved the voice of Paul Robeson, and he had been a great favourite with the Scottish Miners.

Barbara told me that he had been blacklisted because of his connection with Russia and his apparent sympathy for communism.

I explained that the Scottish miners were not all communists but were certainly socialists. I think Barbara was from the South, and for her, the word "socialist" was one step away from evil. Russia, Cuba, and nuclear issues were bad memories for the Americans in the 1960s.

Doc chimed in, saying, "Russia was a bad connection for the man. You cannot fight the State."

Apparently, "Robeson" was quite a famous white slave name in the eighteenth century. I was starting to learn about these things after the great Cassius Clay had dropped his slave's name and become Muhammed Ali.

Many in Scotland just thought Paul Robeson was fighting injustice and for fairness. I had to agree to disagree with

Barbara. The word "fair" means different things to different people. It does not always mean justice.

Something I had been researching for exams in the 1960s was the construction of the Sydney Opera House in Australia. I later saw an article about Paul Robeson singing to the construction workers on the site. He had still been active and making an impact.

Barbara reckoned her roots were not Irish or Scottish, but they, the Irish and Scots, were not any better than the rest of the white settlers. There would be many Black Americans with Scots and Irish names.

Doc was keeping quiet, and Barbara was on a roll. We cannot change the past, but we can only do our best to treat people with respect in the future.

Barbara asked me, "What are you then?"

Now there was a loaded question. In Scotland, if you wanted to know someone's religion, you asked, "What school did you go to?"

I replied, "Well, first and foremost, I am a human being!" It was not the time to explain that I am an Agnostic with Atheist tendencies.

A disappointed Barbara responded, "Is that it?"

I added, "Well, currently, a non-smoking human being."

We got a smile from Barbara and a little laugh from the Doc. It felt like a moment deserving of a rant from one of the Monty Python characters.

I never saw the Coastguard lads again, but I was happy our paths had crossed.

I thought of the conversations with Barbara when I worked on an American Navy base in Mid-Scotland at RAF Edzell. In the mid-1980s. It was a Navy base. Unfortunately,

I never got the chance to speak to one of the Black personnel who had an almost identical surname, with just one vowel changed.

I did make enquiries about the whole topic after I left the project and the island. There's a great slave museum in Liverpool. I would have also told Barbara about a Scot who had worked on the Underground Railway during the abolition of the slavery period. John Hossack House in Ottawa, Illinois. We were certainly not all bad.

We went on one excursion to Unst because one of the Vadil lads, Tim, had read that there was a lone albatross that used to visit the island during the nesting period. We were also going to walk across Hermaness to view the most northerly British Lighthouse, 'Muckle Flugga'.

This was my third time on the island, and once again, the weather was very kind. The lighthouse had been built in 1854, funnily enough when the John Hossack house was being built, through the efforts of Robert Louis Stevenson's uncles. I had a cousin whom I had met once, who for a time had been a lighthouse keeper. Muckle Flugga still had lighthouse keepers at this time, and I can remember thinking it was not a job I would have fancied. Did they suffer from the blues? George Farm, the goalkeeper in the famous Stanley Mathews Cup final of 1953, had spent a short time as a lighthouse keeper in the 1970s.

The walk across Hermaness Nature Reserve was not without problems because it was where there was a large colony of Nesting Skuas. We travelled up in two Land Rovers to the island, including the 12-seater safari.

The route to Muckle Flugga skirted the nesting area, but the Skuas still dive-bombed the rambling group. There were ten of us who had made the trip, and I managed the walk with Roberto (Bob). A Skua is quite a big seabird with a not-too-small beak. We realised the Skuas meant business when one of the lads, Mike, suffered a head injury that required four stitches! The only attraction Mike had was a bald head. We were reminded that all the birds were doing was protecting their young.

When I see the Alfred Hitchcock film, it reminds me of Hermaness. We managed to continue the ramble without further mishaps but did a fair bit of ducking and diving. The view of the Muckle Flugga lighthouse was stunning. I cannot remember the exact timing, but I did witness a youngster, whom I presumed to be a Shetlander, climbing on a different small cliff face not far from where I had played rugby three years before. He wasn't roped up but was carrying a small backpack. It was quite a bit later when I wondered if he was collecting gull's eggs. I remember my old auntie telling me that they did this in her fishing community on the Black Isle before the war. She used the eggs when she was baking, and I was told the baked items had a unique flavour!

When we completed our Muckle Flugga adventure, we returned to seek out the wandering albatross. I still half-believed it was a joke, and that there would be some summer tourist attraction cavorting around shouting, "Albatross, Albatross, Albatross," as per an old Monty Python sketch with a John Cleese lookalike.

The albatross was real, although I never saw it flying, and apparently, it returned to the Shetland cliffs for some 40 years! The expert opinion was that its radar system simply malfunctioned. Maybe it simply wanted to be alone. It certainly never went for the peace because there were plenty of other noisy seabirds nesting.

My last visit to Unst and the Windswept Isles was in 2015, a family holiday that everyone loved. We spent 10 days on the islands, with 7 days on Unst in a superb family home. We also managed to squeeze in a visit to St Ninian's Isle on the main island. It is certainly one of the top beaches in the United Kingdom and also the largest tombolo in the UK. The location is steeped in history, and we visited on a day when the weather was kind. The grandkids were not interested in the history, but the beach was in beautiful condition, surrounded by sparkling blue sea on two sides. I understood what the word 'tombolo' meant and could maybe comprehend what the attraction was for visiting Saints. We had a great day just playing on the beach. It was fairly calm during our visit.

I was lucky because I worked with some excellent people right through my working life and career. I started as an Apprentice Quantity Surveyor in a professional office in Kirkcaldy, Fife in 1965 for Robert Galbraith & Lawson. Robert Galbraith became a pen name for J K Rowling when she started writing her excellent crime novels.

Seeing the name on the bookshelves always remained a tenuous connection to my past.

The holiday was one of our memorable family holidays, and 2015 was a year we remembered fondly. I had a birthday lunch at the Baltasound Hotel and realised that I had managed to work for over 50 years in the Construction Industry. I was still dodging along but only generally working a couple of days a week.

I would have liked to have met a few old faces, but sadly knew that a fair number were no longer with us. Muckle

Flugga was still magnificent but was no longer manned, and Mike, who had been dive-bombed by the Skuas, was retired. I did a fair bit of walking around Unst and spent a day walking around Fetlar.

That same year, I was surprised to receive an invitation to a celebration on board the Britannia, now anchored in Leith. I had resigned my position in 2011 from my old company and was not a fan of the Managing Director or his sidekick. I remember the Queen had been onboard the Britannia when she officially opened the Sullom Voe terminal. It was magnificent to view, but you did not realise how small the cabins were. It was great to catch up with some old faces, including the team from Newcastle. The Managing Director never acknowledged me, but I wasn't going to have a sleepless night worrying about it.

When I became self-employed in 2011, I tended to get involved when people had a few problems or difficulties. I knew 'Subbie Bashing' or 'Subcontractors are sometimes worth more dead than alive' was still on the go. It had been going on for a couple of centuries! At least I could honestly say that I never purposely took that route.

I had been busy working on many other contracts thirty years previously and chasing our own money, so I didn't hear until a couple of weeks later that one of our Ventilation Subcontractors, who told someone that they had cash flow problems, had gone into Administration. I subsequently found out that their cheque had not been posted.

The Mechanical Contract Manager was happy, and he said we would benefit financially from their demise. Our final account costs would now be reduced. It was the first time I can remember hearing the expression, "Sometimes the subcontractor is worth more dead than alive."

I never knew who stopped the cheque, but I wasn't a fan of how it had been engineered. I did have a few companies go bust on us over the years but never pursued a policy of non-payments affecting their cash flow. The biggest problems I was to encounter regarding non-payments were to come from the big players, With Carillion being one of them.

I could remember a couple of my old pals reminding me that Carillion had put more subcontractors out of business than they had hot dinners! There will be many thousands with stories to tell.

I had heard some bad reports about my old company, and I was saddened more than shocked. I knew in my time there we had walked away from Carillion's appalling payment records. I had worked on a few successful Carillion contracts, and there were some good people. However, if you cannot get paid, you walk away. I heard stories from subcontractors but could only give friendly advice. I could not believe that my old company had chosen to tender Carillion contracts.

Historically, I had done a fair bit of travelling throughout the United Kingdom and met some great characters. Northern Island, Newcastle, and Oxfordshire were familiar haunts. The sites were all over the country. My days flying into Luton were long, with seventeen to eighteen hours not unusual. I can remember on one of my first flying visits down south the Berlin Wall was being demolished.

In my last couple of years with my old company, I still had a relationship with my relatively new Contract Manager, Billy McNeil, although it was not always polite. The weather in Central Scotland at the end of 2010 was Baltic, with heavy snow and difficult driving conditions. It made for long, stressful days. The weather continued into 2011. We were now on our third Plumbing Subcontractor on a big school contract in Lanarkshire, and he had done a good job for us. I still had a difference of opinion on the value of their account, but I remained cautious in my reports with Billy.

Billy was not a shy individual, but I was long past being intimidated and could always hold my corner. The cost report was tabled every month, and I can hear Billy saying, "What the fuck is this?"

I would respond, "What's the problem, Billy?"

His response would be along the lines, "Why the fuck are you paying this subcontractor £25,000?"

I responded, "What the fuck are you talking about, Billy? I have not paid that yet. He has £30,000 on cost, which I think is worth £25,000. It may end up a wee bit less than that, but we are all agreed the subbie has done a good job."

Billy said he was still not happy, and I said, "If you are still not fucking happy, change the report and put your name to it."

The report wasn't altered, and I was honestly a little perplexed because we were happy with that subcontractor, and I was led to believe Billy had been invited to a hospitality event with the subcontractor along with the boss.

I heard not long after that the subcontractor had cash flow problems and subsequently was offered a much lower figure which he bitterly accepted. I refused to issue the final account documentation and knew that the end was in sight. He subsequently went into administration, and he was worth more dead than alive! In very simple terms, the account was £25,000 better off, and the word was my boss man got a bonus! There was nothing I could do, and I decided it was time to go. The subcontractor did say he would kill the people involved, and I remember telling him not to go there. We had a couple of long conversations. I did worry, but as the years rolled by, I was glad that threat was not carried out.

It did happen sometimes because I could remember on a site in Edinburgh when my opposite number was threatened by an unhappy subcontractor wielding a gun. The gun wasn't fired, but the subcontractor was jailed.

Could I have done better for my plumbing subcontractor, I asked myself many times.

In 2011, I resigned from my position at the company and became self-employed. I did receive kind words from the family members, but it was time to go. I wasn't happy with the new regime and their new "modus operandi." I was entering the twilight zone and did not have a plan. I still had a couple of years to go before pensions kicked in, but I felt I could survive, and more importantly, get peace of mind.

The company was a family business, and they had a hard core of operatives that had been with them for many years. The labour force in Scotland was excellent, and people were treated with respect. You took pride in your work and did a good job.

There was a family company that I had encountered in Cheshire in the mid-1970s, on a school contract, that I was impressed with who were a family company. Leonard Finney has now passed on, but he always wanted to do a good job and be proud of his work. I met a number of his old employees and tradesmen over the years. He treated them with respect. Why should you not?

What I never envisaged was being threatened, but that was a little foolhardy. If you have to fight to get paid, then you deal with some difficult characters. One client, an excellent family business I worked for over 10 years, had a few truly appalling clients. One who was just a straightforward conman and one who was a high-profile criminal.

My client never received any money from either, and I had advised against the conman. Roughly £80,000 was lost on that contract. The criminal contact was involved in a potential redevelopment of a prestigious site in Fife. The development did not go ahead, but there were materials supplied for other areas. An invoice for under £1,000 was issued by the team, but no payment was received. I was asked to chase the payment, and the call was taken by the company's Managing Director, who I later identified as a convicted criminal.

I did not know his history at that stage, but it was an angry telephone call I could remember, and he told me nobody chased him for money. What was my name, and did I know who I was talking to? Mm.

We sent a recorded delivery letter chasing the debt, and it was the first time in my experience that the letter was not delivered. It was returned a few weeks later by the Post Office!

It was decided that it was not worth chasing the debt through the Smalls Claims Court. My client's client was suspected of being heavily involved in the drug trade, and he was the chief suspect in the murder of his brother-in-law a few years before. The prestigious Fife site was known as an infamous location where drugs were available.

I had been threatened a few times over the years, but I was over fifty years old before I got more heavily involved in some of the legal matters. It was difficult when you were being bullied, but your survival was always an important part of the game, both company-wise and personally.

I had kept fairly good records and still had my interpretation of "The Good, the Bad & the Nasty."

I had a run-in with Barratt Homes in North Wales in the mid-1970s on a site in Cheshire when their famous Helicopter man, Patrick Allen, was doing all the television adverts. I had given them a price which their Welsh Director accepted, and we got the go-ahead to finish several homes. The mistake I made, and it was the last time I committed that error, was that we did not get the acceptance in writing! When we had completed the work, my Welsh Director stated we were too expensive, and the resident teams were doing it cheaper!

He was 100% correct because my teams had noticed that the 'Resident Teams' were never on site on Thursdays, which, as it turned out, was their day for signing on at the Unemployment Bureau, affectionately known as the 'Dole'. His teams were what at the time was called 'On the Grip'. There was no way you could compete with that. Some you win and some you lose.

My memory recalled when we had won a fairly prestigious Edinburgh hotel contract for a top Edinburgh Contractor, but only electrically, in the late 1990s. One of our competitors had won the Mechanical contract. We had completed several contracts for them successfully elsewhere, so potentially we did not see a problem. In the previous decade, I had worked with a different team that completed another electrical contract at Stirling Royal Infirmary. My only sad footnote on that contract was the Health Board demolished a lot of that building just a few years later. We did, unfortunately, have one major problem before we started the hotel contract because we had won a very big contract elsewhere, there was a shortage of labour. It was not unusual for a labourer to be hired by one of your competitors, especially if they had some surplus labour. The only problem was that the labour came from one of the Main Contractor's subsidiary companies.

I got on well with my opposite number, Brian, but you still have to remember the relationship. You work hard and do the business to make sure you get paid every month. I heard criticism of Brian from another senior source who was someone I didn't trust. About ten years later, he was to become our new Managing Director. The word "fair" was sometimes seen as weak.

The contract never got off to a good start, and sadly, it never recovered. It was the first time that we had a contractual dispute that went legal. The Construction Industry had strong characters, and that simply led to straightforward bullying.

We had an incident on-site one day. I had a very busy schedule and regularly worked long hours, so I was doing well if I was on this specific site once a week. I was asked to a meeting in the Main Contractors Site office. "Asked" was maybe the wrong word, but I was instructed to attend a meeting to discuss inadequacies and poor performance!

Our Electrical Director, Contract Manager, and Engineer were not available, but I was informed that we had not received any written confirmation of defects or poor workmanship in preparing the ground for the alleged contra charges. The contra charges were reasons to reduce our next-account interim payment. I knew things were not right because I was still having a surreal conversation with one of their background/head office staff who was questioning the cost of a £10,000 variation and said it was worthless. The lad I was dealing with on-site kept out of the discussion.

We had won a competitive tender bid, but when the order was being placed, we were instructed in writing to omit this item valued at £10,000. The order was formally issued, we signed and returned it, and work started a couple of months later. A few months after that, an architect's instruction was issued formally instructing that this item be included in the contract again.

The head office staff member said that there was a gentleman's agreement, and everyone knew that this item was always going to be included. They were not being paid, and therefore we should not expect payment ourselves. I never swore at the person involved but realised that we were on a very difficult journey.

I wish I had been able to record the meeting I did attend on-site because there were certainly no minutes going to be issued.

There were five people from the main contractor and me in the meeting. The main man did all the talking, and there were no pleasantries. He said our company was nothing but a pile of shite and no fucking good to man or beast! The rant went on longer than that! The person, Brian, I dealt with just sat stony—faced, and I did not have any idea what was coming. There was already a spurious reason for non-payment of £10,000. Brian's young assistant, a recent graduate straight out of university, had been given the task of compiling the contra charges. There was a huge pile of work, and just a glance at the top one could tell there were thousands of pounds involved. Could the day get any worse?

As the young man nervously started to read the first alleged contra charge, I couldn't believe my luck. I did feel for him in the position he was in, but I did enjoy my response to the main man. The mistake was 100% incompetence. We were a Mechanical and Electrical company but largely known as a Mechanical Company, which was accounted for 80% of our business. However, on this contract, we had only won the Electrical contract. The contra charges were against the Mechanical Subcontractor!

I said to the boss, "do you realise we are only the fucking Electrical Subcontractor on this contract?"

In the cold light of day, that was a mistake. I was still a lowly subcontractor waiting to get paid. I got up to leave, and Brian said.

"Isn't it time you fucking retired, Dave?"

We were never actually served with detailed contra charge notices.

The Mechanical Contractor did go bust a wee bit further down the line in a blaze involving another famous Edinburgh contractor.

In 1994, The Housing Regeneration Act was passed, with the Scottish version coming shortly after, and it had a huge impact on subcontractors because it improved payment practices. It became illegal to include a 'Pay when paid' clause in your contract. Not everyone was happy about this change, especially many of them main contractors and perhaps a few clients.

In terms of sports, 1994 was a memorable year for me because my team, Raith Rovers, unexpectedly defeated Celtic in the Scottish League Cup final, which was sponsored by Coca-Cola. The victory was a pleasant surprise for our team and supporters. The crowd sang an old Fife folk song called 'Geordie Munro', and David Latto's twenty-first century version of the song was superb. However, in early 1994, the world witnessed the Rwandan genocide, a tragic event on the African continent.

The electrical contract on the aforementioned prestigious Edinburgh hotel happened a few years after 1994. The dispute led to us taking the contract to Adjudication, which is a simplified legal process to recover payment. I heard through the grapevine that at least three other subcontractors who were taking similar actions on this contract.

Brian's boss, Paul, whom I vaguely knew, pulled me aside at one occasion to have a quiet word. I knew of his reputation, and he was a respected professional from my part of the world. I will always remember the gist of the conversation where he said, "Listen, Dave, we do have a problem with this contract because the client isn't paying us."

I can also remember my response was not rude; I said.

"Paul, I can sympathise with that problem, but you know that the 1996 act has made that defence illegal."

We had these discussions before we pressed the adjudication button, and I do remember the phone call from Paul surprised that we had chosen this route and asking if we would reconsider.

What I didn't mention at the time that I had received reliable information suggesting that he was being paid by the client on a different contract. However, I still hadn't forgotten I was a subcontractor and knew I couldn't press that button.

I could imagine Paul doing his best Jeffrey Archer's impression in the witness box, holding up his right hand and saying, "I swear to tell the truth, the whole truth, and nothing like the truth, so help me God."

The adjudication proceeded in our lawyers' Edinburgh office, and it was a nerve—wracking experience. Thoughts of potential redundancies and the survival of our business weighed heavily. There were six of us around the table: the Adjudicator, Paul, Brian, the Site Agent, our Electrical Director, and myself.

The Adjudicator had a very serious job to do, and the session atmosphere was very strained. Although there was no jocularity, he reminded me of a great Scottish comic actor Rikki Fulton in his role as the Reverend I. M. Jolly. He played a similar role as a Russian major in the film 'Gorky Park', starring William Hurt and Lee Marvin. I had the good fortune to see him on stage with his good buddy Jack Milroy not long before that.

Looking back, I couldn't help but wonder if Lee Marvin's song, 'I Was Born Under a Wandering Star', would have been an appropriate soundtrack for that surreal session.

We had a slight difference of opinion with our team regarding our submission. My Director wanted me to rescind any agreements that had been reached with Brian, my opposite number during the contract. It wasn't an order, but I believed, as per my brief appearance in Aberdeen Sheriff's Court as an expert witness, that in these situations, you play it with a straight bat. You tell the truth because the person asking the question usually already knows the answer. There was no swearing on oath, and you simply answered the Adjudicator's questions.

The only time I noticed a faint glimmer of expression from the Adjudicator was when one of his eyebrows flicked upon hearing that the building team could not give anything like a genuine reason why a straightforward site instruction had not been paid. I thought the Adjudicator, much like the Reverend I. M. Jolly, would have made a good poker player.

We didn't wait too long to hear the news. I was a little disappointed with the award figure. We were awarded £75,000, but when I read the notification in-depth, it was clear that further items had to be resolved. Our lawyer was very pleased because the most important aspect was that the Adjudicator awarded all costs against our client.

Unbelievably, the account was settled within a couple of weeks at approximately a further £225,000. We still had a further 12 months of the Defects period to run, but we continued to fulfil our contractual obligations.

One thing you don't do is win an adjudication. You get a result. We never worked for them again in my time with the company, and our name was Mud. They were a big company, and obviously, you are off their tender list.

I never truly understood the full picture of what happened in this contract. I subsequently heard there were more adjudications. I heard that they had a major structural/engineering problem with the contract. What was the relationship with the client? The strange start with the £10,000 query item. The hotel was converted to flats later on.

I was involved in a further three adjudications, all from different offices, and they were not hard work but very time-consuming when you are trying to carry out your normal business. It also meant, for some time, I was fairly involved with our lawyers, Jim and June, who I thought did a great job. Lawyers don't come cheap, but I was not criticising. It just puts pressure on your budgets. Modern technology with computers and e-mails increased the pressure.

I can remember getting a communication at 21:00 hours one Saturday night in June when we had a deadline to meet. I never met any of the other adjudicators and never visited the sites. We got three results, and in the short term, that was all that mattered. One of the adjudications in England was taken to court, but the court backed the adjudicator. I could read about that on the internet but realised it was well out of my league.

I was introduced to a self-employed joiner, Bob, who was unable to get paid from his client for work he had done in a house in Perthshire. I said I would look at the paperwork and give an honest opinion. He worked from home, and you could quickly see that he appeared to be genuine. His client was a Chartered Surveyor who worked for one of the local councils. He had gotten the work done, and because Bob was doing a good job, he had him do additional work. He then said the work was substandard, and Bob's invoice was rejected! He wasn't going to pay.

We tried sending recorded delivery letters, but they were answered unsympathetically. It was clear there was to be no compromise. My client, Bob, and his wife decided that they were not going to walk away. They were a great couple, and they just wanted justice. We served the appropriate papers to take the case to the small claims court in Perth. We all turned up in court, and the case was to be dealt within a few weeks' time at a specific date given to us by the court.

My client, in the intervening period, was offered a settlement figure in the four-figure sum but rejected it. When we finally turned up in court for the final session, I thought our gentleman adversary, a Chartered Surveyor, would at least present some photographs or maybe swear those immortal lines, "I swear to tell the truth, the whole truth, and nothing like the truth, so help me God."

It didn't happen; our Chartered Surveyor conceded. The case was not tested in court, and our opponent stated he had cash flow problems.

Bob and his wife were vindicated.

I sent a few recorded delivery letters to various names for different reasons. I never knew all the reasons, but I just dealt with the simple facts. One was to a TV star, and my client had his invoice paid within 10 days. A client argued with a company where I noticed Winston Churchill's grandson, Sir Nicholas Soames, was a director. The client was getting the "deaf ear" treatment, so I sent a recorded delivery letter to the House of Commons. I never got a reply, but the problem was resolved. A little bit later, I came across an excellent book called "Cheers Mr Churchill" written by Andrew Liddle.

One of my favourite sayings that Winston Churchill borrowed from Mark Twain was, "There are lies, damned lies, and statistics."

I'm not sure that so many of his sayings would be appreciated in the twenty-first century, but I still agreed with, "We make a living by what we get, we make a life but what we give."

It sounded like it was one step away from socialism! My dad had a slightly different saying at the start of the First World War, "You had to work to eat."

Winston Churchill was still a great Prime Minister and the right man in the right place in 1939.

Never thought I would see another war in Europe, and the talk is at least half a million casualties. One of my Shetland three musketeers had recently passed away, but we still remembered the happy memories. Different statistics.

I could remember the rationing in the 1950s and the street party in Glasswork Street for the Queen's coronation in 1953. The street where I was born and so was Sandford Fleming, the inventor who promoted worldwide time zones and the twenty-four-hour clock, although he is less well-remembered than Adam Smith. That was the same year that Sir John Hunt led the expedition that conquered Everest. Strangely, I encountered Sir John 10 years later at an International camp in Glenalmond, Perthshire.

Glasswork Street is still there, but there is very little to see now that all the tenements are demolished, and I could not imagine a street party being held there. The lemonade works, also demolished, used to be opposite the tenement buildings where my friend Jimmy and I pinched a few lemonade bottles from the back of their lorry. I was eight years old and in the bad books for a long time. I never wandered down that path again.

There were so many happy memories throughout my working life, which enabled us to survive and enjoy family life. I had the good fortune to work all over the United Kingdom, and I could not talk negatively about any parts of the islands. Good people everywhere just trying to get on with their lives. I had told the story of my dad being rescued by the Clacton-On-Sea lifeboat in 1917, and you realise what selfless communities do throughout the country. A cousin had been involved in the Cromarty lifeboat rescue in the 1950s, and Dad was so proud to read about it in the papers. My old pal

Bob, who I met in Shetland, was involved with the New Brighton lifeboat on the Wirral.

I read an article on Chad Varah in Shetland in 1978, and it was the first time I realised that he was instrumental in setting up the Samaritans in 1953. The story of a young 14-year-old girl who took her own life is unbelievably sad. He did amazing work, and I could not disagree with his ethos that it is better to give than to receive.

I would have loved to see the Reverend Chad Varah communicating with Charles Dickens if there was an afterlife.

"Always look on the bright side of life" was one of our singalong songs on the Rangatira, one of the accommodation ships in Shetland for the first oil ashore. That was a different story.